ADVENT AND CHRISTMAS 2024

SACREDSPACE
1 DECEMBER 2024 TO 11 JANUARY 2025

FROM THE WEBSITE WWW.SACREDSPACE.IE
PRAYER FROM THE IRISH JESUITS

Published by Messenger Publications, 2025

Copyright © the Irish Jesuits, 2025

The right of the Irish Jesuits to be identified as the author of the Work has been asserted by them in accordance with the Copyright and Related Rights Act, 2000. All rights reserved. No part of this book may be reproduced or utilised in any form or by any means electronic or mechanical including photography, filming, recording, video recording, photocopying or by any information storage and retrieval system or shall not by way of trade or otherwise be lent, resold or otherwise circulated in any form of binding or cover other than that in which it is published without prior permission in writing from the publisher.

Scripture quotations are taken from the New Revised Standard Version Updated Edition. Copyright © 2021 National Council of Churches of Christ in the United States of America. Used by permission. All rights reserved worldwide.

Weekly reflections are taken from books and periodicals published by Messenger Publications. For more information go to www.messenger.ie.

ISBN: 978 1 78812 701 1

Designed by Brendan McCarthy
Typeset in Adobe Caslon Pro & Avant Garde
Printed by Hussar Books

Messenger Publications,
37 Leeson Place,
Dublin D02 E5V0,
Ireland
www.messenger.ie

How to Use This Booklet

During each week of Advent, begin by reading the 'Something to think and pray about each day this week'. Then go through 'the Presence of God', 'Freedom' and 'Consciousness' steps to help you prepare yourself to hear the Word of God speaking to you. In the next step, 'The Word', turn to the Scripture reading for each day of the week. Inspiration points are provided if you need them. Then return to the 'conversation' and 'conclusion' steps. Follow this process every day of Advent.

The Advent retreat at the back of this book follows a similar structure: an invitation to experience stillness, a Scripture passage and reflection points, and suggestions for prayer; you may find it useful to move back and forth between the daily reflections and the retreat.

The First Week of Advent

1–7 December 2024

Something to think and pray about each day this week:

Advent is a time to remind ourselves of the many contradictions at the heart of our faith. This most powerful presence chose to be manifest in powerlessness.

As we prepare to celebrate the moment the Word became flesh our faith needs deepening. Ours is a faith that sincerely accepts the darkness surrounding the search for more light. Consequently, Advent is a time of loving adoration, a true act of supernatural hope and of loving surrender to this shy God.

This shy God reminds us this Advent that life is about relationships, not about things. The greatest joy comes from good relationships – the greatest sorrow and suffering come not from loss of job or property but from broken and betrayed relationships. All relationships of love are rooted in the love this shy God has for all of us.

Vincent Sherlock, *Let Advent be Advent*

CONTENTS

Sacred Space Prayer 4

How to Use This Booklet 5

The First Week of Advent 6

The Second Week of Advent 17

The Third Week of Advent 27

The Fourth Week of Advent/Christmas 41

The First Week of Christmas 53

The Second Week of Christmas 65

An Advent Retreat 78

Reflection for Advent 94

Sacred Space Prayer

Bless all who worship you, almighty God,
from the rising of the sun to its setting;
from your goodness enrich us,
by your love inspire us,
by your Spirit guide us,
by your power protect us,
in your mercy receive us,
now and always.

The Presence of God
'Be still, and know that I am God.' Lord, your words lead us to the calmness and greatness of your presence.

Freedom
I am free. When I look at these words in writing, they seem to create in me a feeling of awe. Yes, a wonderful feeling of freedom. Thank you, God.

Consciousness
At this moment, Lord, I turn my thoughts to you.
I will leave aside my chores and preoccupations.
I will take rest and refreshment in your presence, Lord.

The Word
The word of God comes down to us through the Scriptures. May the Holy Spirit enlighten my mind and my heart to respond to the Gospel teachings. (*Please turn to the Scripture on the following pages. Inspiration points are there, should you need them. When you are ready, return here to continue.*)

Conversation
Begin to talk with Jesus about the Scripture you have just read. What part of it strikes a chord in you? Perhaps the words of a friend – or some story you have heard recently – will slowly rise to the surface of

your consciousness. If so, does the story throw light on what the Scripture passage may be trying to say to you?

Conclusion
Glory be to the Father, and to the Son, and to the Holy Spirit,
As it was in the beginning, is now and ever shall be,
World without end. Amen.

Sunday 1 December
First Sunday of Advent
Luke 21:25–28.34–36

'There will be signs in the sun, the moon, and the stars, and on the earth distress among nations confused by the roaring of the sea and the waves. People will faint from fear and foreboding of what is coming upon the world, for the powers of the heavens will be shaken. Then they will see "the Son of Man coming in a cloud" with power and great glory. Now when these things begin to take place, stand up and raise your heads, because your redemption is drawing near.'

'Be on guard so that your hearts are not weighed down with dissipation and drunkenness and the worries of this life, and that day does not catch you unexpectedly, like a trap. For it will come upon all who live on the face of the whole earth. Be alert at all times, praying that you may have the strength to escape all these things that will take place, and to stand before the Son of Man.'

- In Advent we are to prepare to celebrate the coming of our saviour Jesus Christ into our world as one of us. St Luke advises us to so live that we can stand with confidence before our God when he comes a second time to judge the world. May this time of Advent be for us a time of renewal and a deeper faith.
- Our God is always inviting us to come to him and to place him at the centre of our lives. Do I always

put him in the first place in my life? God can never take second place.

Monday 2 December
Matthew 8:5–11
When he entered Capernaum, a centurion came to him, appealing to him and saying, 'Lord, my servant is lying at home paralysed, in terrible distress.' And he said to him, 'I will come and cure him.' The centurion answered, 'Lord, I am not worthy to have you come under my roof; but only speak the word, and my servant will be healed. For I also am a man under authority, with soldiers under me; and I say to one, "Go", and he goes, and to another, "Come", and he comes, and to my slave, "Do this", and the slave does it.' When Jesus heard him, he was amazed and said to those who followed him, 'Truly I tell you, in no one in Israel have I found such faith. I tell you, many will come from east and west and will eat with Abraham and Isaac and Jacob in the kingdom of heaven.'

- In this foreigner who comes to Jesus we have one of the best examples of faith we can find in the gospels. We recall it in every Mass as we are preparing to receive our Lord in communion.
- It brought great joy to Jesus whenever he encountered faith in those he met as with this centurion. To doubting Thomas he said, 'You believe because you

can see me. Blessed are those who have not seen and yet believe.' Lord, help me to grow in my faith by using whatever little faith I have. In our prayer now we can give him this great joy by believing him and trusting in him.

Tuesday 3 December
Luke 10:21–24
At that same hour Jesus rejoiced in the Holy Spirit and said, 'I thank you, Father, Lord of heaven and earth, because you have hidden these things from the wise and the intelligent and have revealed them to infants; yes, Father, for such was your gracious will. All things have been handed over to me by my Father; and no one knows who the Son is except the Father, or who the Father is except the Son and anyone to whom the Son chooses to reveal him.'

Then turning to the disciples, Jesus said to them privately, 'Blessed are the eyes that see what you see! For I tell you that many prophets and kings desired to see what you see, but did not see it, and to hear what you hear, but did not hear it.'

- Jesus is always the best model to teach us how we should pray. He simply speaks from his heart to his beloved Father using his own words in whatever situation he finds himself in. Let us learn from the Master and speak from our hearts to him who is here with us.

- Unlike those 'many prophets and kings', we have the benefit of Christ's example and his words. Let us take the advice of St Teresa of Avila and look at him with eyes of faith and recall that the Holy Spirit is dwelling within us.

Wednesday 4 December
Matthew 15:29–37

After Jesus had left that place, he passed along the Sea of Galilee, and he went up the mountain, where he sat down. Great crowds came to him, bringing with them the lame, the maimed, the blind, the mute, and many others. They put them at his feet, and he cured them, so that the crowd was amazed when they saw the mute speaking, the maimed whole, the lame walking, and the blind seeing. And they praised the God of Israel.

Then Jesus called his disciples to him and said, 'I have compassion for the crowd, because they have been with me now for three days and have nothing to eat; and I do not want to send them away hungry, for they might faint on the way.' The disciples said to him, 'Where are we to get enough bread in the desert to feed so great a crowd?' Jesus asked them, 'How many loaves have you?' They said, 'Seven, and a few small fish.' Then ordering the crowd to sit down on the ground, he took the seven loaves and the fish; and after giving thanks he broke them and gave them to the disciples, and the disciples gave them to the crowds. And all of them ate and were filled; and they took up the broken pieces left over, seven baskets full.

- Jesus always had compassion for the crowds that came to hear him. He feeds them first through his preaching on the level of their spirits, and then he looks after their bodily needs. Jesus said, 'My words are spirit and they are life.' Let us take his words into our hearts and respond to them with whatever words come to mind.
- Jesus is still our Shepherd today and in prayer we can be in his company. We can now take the words of Psalm 22, 'The Lord is my Shepherd', and allow them to speak to us, responding with whatever comes to mind.

Thursday 5 December
Matthew 7:21.24–27

Then Jesus said to his disciples, 'Not everyone who says to me, "Lord, Lord", will enter the kingdom of heaven, but only one who does the will of my Father in heaven.

'Everyone then who hears these words of mine and acts on them will be like a wise man who built his house on rock. The rain fell, the floods came, and the winds blew and beat on that house, but it did not fall, because it had been founded on rock. And everyone who hears these words of mine and does not act on them will be like a foolish man who built his house on sand. The rain fell, and the floods came, and the winds blew and beat against that house, and it fell – and great was its fall!'

- When Jesus was told his family were outside and wanted to speak to him, he replied by saying his family are those who do the will of his Father. So not one who says 'Lord, Lord' … Love is proved by deeds not words. Jesus said, 'Do not pray like the pagans do, who think that they will be heard for their many words.' You may wish now to speak simply with the Lord in your own words about whatever is going on in your life.
- If we build our lives and our faith on the rock that is Christ no storms can overcome us. May we be filled with confidence when Jesus tells us, 'Take courage, I have overcome the world.' By his life, death and resurrection he has won for us every grace we will ever need.

Friday 6 December
Matthew 9:27–31

As Jesus went on from there, two blind men followed him, crying loudly, 'Have mercy on us, Son of David!' When he entered the house, the blind men came to him; and Jesus said to them, 'Do you believe that I am able to do this?' They said to him, 'Yes, Lord.' Then he touched their eyes and said, 'According to your faith let it be done to you.' And their eyes were opened. Then Jesus sternly ordered them, 'See that no one knows of this.' But they went away and spread the news about him throughout that district.

- As the two blind men continue to plead with Jesus he appears to ignore them. Yet he still grants them their request. Every prayer we make is heard by God, but for our good he often delays his response to our petitions. By persevering in prayer our faith grows stronger. We pray for this grace.
- Jesus, you told us to ask for all our needs. May we trust in your unchanging love for us. You always know what is best for us.

Saturday 7 December
Matthew 9:35–10:1.5.6–8
Then Jesus went about all the cities and villages, teaching in their synagogues, and proclaiming the good news of the kingdom, and curing every disease and every sickness. When he saw the crowds, he had compassion for them, because they were harassed and helpless, like sheep without a shepherd. Then he said to his disciples, 'The harvest is plentiful, but the labourers are few; therefore ask the Lord of the harvest to send out labourers into his harvest.'

Then Jesus summoned his twelve disciples and gave them authority over unclean spirits, to cast them out, and to cure every disease and every sickness.

These twelve Jesus sent out with the following instructions: 'Go nowhere among the Gentiles, and enter no town of the Samaritans, but go rather to the lost sheep of the house of Israel. As you go, proclaim the good news, "The kingdom of heaven has come near." Cure the sick, raise the dead, cleanse the lepers, cast out demons. You received without payment; give without payment.'

- In his compassion and love, Jesus continues to sustain and love all people, and he wants them to come to know him. 'I have come that they may have life and have it to the full.' Jesus knew that in his humanity he could not reach every place and that after his death and his return to his Father he would need his apostles and his disciples, namely us, to bring the Good News to his people.
- Pope Francis reminds us that each of us has a mission. We are to witness to our God by how we live. 'Lord, help us to live our faith in accordance with your will.'

The Second Week of Advent

8–14 December 2024

Something to think and pray about each day this week:

During this time of the year, I notice myself withdrawing from the busy pace of the world to seek quiet time for reflection. Nature is integral to my daily spiritual life. In the sacred space of the natural world, I feel a profound sense of what it means to be part of the web of life – to belong to a bigger cosmic consciousness.

A nature-based approach to spirituality could hold the solution to our feelings of alienation and disconnection from the Church, our global community and even our role in the current global climate change crisis. As we make it our intention to restore this connection in order to overcome the current socio-ecological crises that threaten our survival as a species on the planet, we also deepen our own faith. As Thomas Berry wisely observed, 'The destiny of humans cannot be separated from the destiny of the earth.'

Andrea Hayes, *The Sacred Heart Messenger*, December 2021

The Presence of God
'Come to me, all you who are weary and are carrying heavy burdens, and I will give you rest.' Here I am, Lord. I come to seek your presence. I long for your healing power.

Freedom
'In these days, God taught me as a schoolteacher teaches a pupil' (St Ignatius). I remind myself that there are things God has to teach me yet, and I ask for the grace to hear those things and let them change me.

Consciousness
Help me, Lord, to be more conscious of your presence. Teach me to recognise your presence in others. Fill my heart with gratitude for the times your love has been shown to me through the care of others.

The Word
God speaks to each of us individually. I listen attentively to hear what he is saying to me. Read the text a few times, then listen. (*Please turn to the Scripture on the following pages. Inspiration points are there, should you need them. When you are ready, return here to continue.*)

Conversation
Conversation requires talking and listening.
As I talk to Jesus, may I also learn to be still and listen.
I picture the gentleness in his eyes and the smile full of love as he gazes on me.
I can be totally honest with Jesus as I tell him of my worries and my cares.
I will open my heart to him as I tell him of my fears and my doubts.
I will ask him to help me place myself fully in his care and to abandon myself to him, knowing that he always wants what is best for me.

Conclusion
I thank God for these moments we have spent together and for any insights I have been given concerning the text.

Sunday 8 December
Second Sunday of Advent
Luke 3:1–6

In the fifteenth year of the reign of Emperor Tiberius, when Pontius Pilate was governor of Judea, and Herod was ruler of Galilee, and his brother Philip ruler of the region of Ituraea and Trachonitis, and Lysanias ruler of Abilene, during the high-priesthood of Annas and Caiaphas, the word of God came to John son of Zechariah in the wilderness. He went into all the region around the Jordan, proclaiming a baptism of repentance for the forgiveness of sins, as it is written in the book of the words of the prophet Isaiah,

'The voice of one crying out in the wilderness:
"Prepare the way of the Lord,
 make his paths straight.
Every valley shall be filled,
 and every mountain and hill shall be made low,
and the crooked shall be made straight,
 and the rough ways made smooth;
and all flesh shall see the salvation of God."'

- St Luke, writing for the Gentile world, announces the beginning of the public ministry of John the Baptist, the last of the prophets before Christ. He is to prepare the way for the Messiah through hearts

that are purified by their repentance for their sins. Only hearts that have turned away from sinful ways can receive the message of the Good News.
- John the Baptist attracts a large following by his preaching and by his witnessing to a simple and austere life. Are we willing to make changes in our lifestyle to be more open to the message of Christ?

Monday 9 December
The Immaculate Conception of the Bvm
Luke 1:26–38
In the sixth month the angel Gabriel was sent by God to a town in Galilee called Nazareth, to a virgin engaged to a man whose name was Joseph, of the house of David. The virgin's name was Mary. And he came to her and said, 'Greetings, favoured one! The Lord is with you.' But she was much perplexed by his words and pondered what sort of greeting this might be. The angel said to her, 'Do not be afraid, Mary, for you have found favour with God. And now, you will conceive in your womb and bear a son, and you will name him Jesus. He will be great, and will be called the Son of the Most High, and the Lord God will give to him the throne of his ancestor David. He will reign over the house of Jacob for ever, and of his kingdom there will be no end.' Mary said to the angel, 'How can this be, since I am a virgin?' The angel said to her, 'The Holy Spirit will come upon

you, and the power of the Most High will overshadow you; therefore the child to be born will be holy; he will be called Son of God. And now, your relative Elizabeth in her old age has also conceived a son; and this is the sixth month for her who was said to be barren. For nothing will be impossible with God.' Then Mary said, 'Here am I, the servant of the Lord; let it be with me according to your word.' Then the angel departed from her.

- Mary was chosen by God for her great role as Christ's Mother, but she is left free in how she will respond to the angel's message. She becomes, by her faith, her trust and her charity, the model for all Christians. She is truly the servant of God in all the ways she cares for and loves her Son.
- Next to Jesus, Mary is the holiest person who has ever lived on this earth. We give thanks to God for the honour bestowed through her upon the whole human race, and ask for the grace to follow her example.

Tuesday 10 December
Matthew 18:12–14
Jesus said to them, 'What do you think? If a shepherd has a hundred sheep, and one of them has gone astray, does he not leave the ninety-nine on the mountains and go in search of the one that went astray? And if

he finds it, truly I tell you, he rejoices over it more than over the ninety-nine that never went astray. So it is not the will of your Father in heaven that one of these little ones should be lost.'

- The theme of God as the Shepherd of his people Israel and the people of God as his flock is very strong in both the Old and New Testaments. Psalm 22 is entirely devoted to it. In John's Gospel it is a major theme and there Jesus says he will lay down his life for his sheep.
- It is clear that our God is a God of mercy. As we look back over our lives let us give him thanks for his many mercies shown to us.

Wednesday 11 December
Matthew 11:28–30

Jesus said, 'Come to me, all you that are weary and are carrying heavy burdens, and I will give you rest. Take my yoke upon you, and learn from me; for I am gentle and humble in heart, and you will find rest for your souls. For my yoke is easy, and my burden is light.'

- What is God like? The apostle Philip once asked Jesus to show them the Father. Jesus replied by saying, 'Have I been with you all this time and you still do not know me? To have seen me is to have seen the Father.' Jesus came to reveal the Father to us.

- In our prayer we share our joys, our sorrows and our hopes with Jesus, this friend who is gentle and humble of heart. 'Truly I have set my soul in silence and peace. As a child has rest in its mother's arms, even so is my soul' (Psalm 131).

Thursday 12 December
Matthew 11:11–15

Jesus said to them, 'Truly I tell you, among those born of women no one has arisen greater than John the Baptist; yet the least in the kingdom of heaven is greater than he. From the days of John the Baptist until now the kingdom of heaven has suffered violence, and the violent take it by force. For all the prophets and the law prophesied until John came; and if you are willing to accept it, he is Elijah who is to come. Let anyone with ears listen!'

- John the Baptist's preaching came at the end of the Old Testament and as the New Testament was about to begin with the life, death and resurrection of Jesus. We have the greater privilege of living in the era of the New Testament and with the witness of the example of a multitude of saints and martyrs in over two thousand years of Christianity. However, we still have to struggle to attain the kingdom of heaven.

- We have the gift of the Holy Spirit given to us and to our Church. How well do we use these gifts that we have received?

Friday 13 December
Matthew 11:16–19
Jesus said to them, 'But to what will I compare this generation? It is like children sitting in the market-places and calling to one another,

"We played the flute for you, and you did not dance;
we wailed, and you did not mourn."

For John came neither eating nor drinking, and they say, "He has a demon"; the Son of Man came eating and drinking, and they say, "Look, a glutton and a drunkard, a friend of tax-collectors and sinners!" Yet wisdom is vindicated by her deeds.'

- The people in Judea and Galilee were given an extraordinary opportunity, as their God walked among them and worked great wonders. For centuries people had longed to see what they saw, to hear what they heard. But in the hardness of their hearts their leaders shut the eyes of their minds to it. There are none so blind as those who do not want to see.
- How open am I to the message of the Good News? Do I take the means to grow in my understanding of it and to know the Lord more and more?

Saturday 14 December
Matthew 17:10–13

And the disciples asked him, 'Why, then, do the scribes say that Elijah must come first?' He replied, 'Elijah is indeed coming and will restore all things; but I tell you that Elijah has already come, and they did not recognise him, but they did to him whatever they pleased. So also the Son of Man is about to suffer at their hands.' Then the disciples understood that he was speaking to them about John the Baptist.

- John the Baptist was seen by many as a great prophet and as Elijah returned in some way. In his ministry he brought a reminder of the old prophecies as he prepared the way for the eventual fulfilment of those prophecies.
- Jesus knew that they would treat him as they had treated the prophets of old. Talk to him now about what it was like to carry within him the burden of this knowledge as he went about his mission in the face of opposition.

Third Week of Advent

15–21 December 2024

Something to think and pray about each day this week:

Like the shepherds, we are invited to step out of our everyday life with its challenges and worries, and 'go now to Bethlehem'; to meet the child Jesus in the manger in all his newness and human vulnerability. We live in a world that can feel increasingly uncertain, dark and frightening. It is important to be engaged, but the barrage of bad news can leave us feeling anxious about the future and about the security of ourselves and our loved ones. This Christmas Day, we have an opportunity, like the shepherds, to step out of our routine and visit the Christmas crib. We bring our worries and anxieties, and perhaps we can leave them there a while as, like Mary, we reflect deeply and treasure this mystery of God with us. The world will still be there to return to, as it was for the shepherds, with a new perspective and renewed hope.

Tríona Doherty and Jane Mellett, *The Deep End: A Journey with the Sunday Gospels in the Year of Mark*

The Presence of God
'I am standing at the door, knocking,' says the Lord. What a wonderful privilege that the Lord of all creation desires to come to me. I welcome his presence.

Freedom
Leave me here freely all alone. / In cell where never sunlight shone. / Should no one ever speak to me. / This golden silence makes me free!

– Part of a poem written by a prisoner at Dachau concentration camp

Consciousness
How am I really feeling? Lighthearted? Heavyhearted? I may be very much at peace, happy to be here. Equally, I may be frustrated, worried or angry. I acknowledge how I really am. It is the real me whom the Lord loves.

The Word
I take my time to read the word of God slowly, a few times, allowing myself to dwell on anything that strikes me. (*Please turn to the Scripture on the following pages. Inspiration points are there, should you need them. When you are ready, return here to continue.*)

Conversation
Do I notice myself reacting as I pray with the word of God? Do I feel challenged, comforted, angry? Imagining Jesus sitting or standing by me, I speak out my feelings, as one trusted friend to another.

Conclusion
Glory be to the Father, and to the Son, and to the Holy Spirit,
As it was in the beginning, is now and ever shall be,
World without end. Amen.

Sunday 15 December
Third Sunday of Advent
Luke 3:10–18

And the crowds asked him, 'What then should we do?' In reply he said to them, 'Whoever has two coats must share with anyone who has none; and whoever has food must do likewise.' Even tax-collectors came to be baptised, and they asked him, 'Teacher, what should we do?' He said to them, 'Collect no more than the amount prescribed for you.' Soldiers also asked him, 'And we, what should we do?' He said to them, 'Do not extort money from anyone by threats or false accusation, and be satisfied with your wages.'

As the people were filled with expectation, and all were questioning in their hearts concerning John, whether he might be the Messiah, John answered all of them by saying, 'I baptise you with water; but one who is more powerful than I is coming; I am not worthy to untie the thong of his sandals. He will baptise you with the Holy Spirit and fire. His winnowing-fork is in his hand, to clear his threshing-floor and to gather the wheat into his granary; but the chaff he will burn with unquenchable fire.'

So, with many other exhortations, he proclaimed the good news to the people.

- As they listened to John the Baptist's call for repentance his hearers rightly asked what change they needed to make in their lives. In his reply the

law of charity came first, as he urged them to share with the poor and to deal honestly with all. Lord, may we show our love by our care for and treatment of others.
- John the Baptist in his humility acknowledges that he is not worthy even to untie our Lord's sandals. We are all called to grow in humility and to acknowledge our own littleness and our complete dependence on our God. We ask God to reveal this more and more to us.

Monday 16 December
Matthew 21:23–27
When he entered the temple, the chief priests and the elders of the people came to him as he was teaching, and said, 'By what authority are you doing these things, and who gave you this authority?' Jesus said to them, 'I will also ask you one question; if you tell me the answer, then I will also tell you by what authority I do these things. Did the baptism of John come from heaven, or was it of human origin?' And they argued with one another, 'If we say, "From heaven", he will say to us, "Why then did you not believe him?" But if we say, "Of human origin", we are afraid of the crowd; for all regard John as a prophet.' So they answered Jesus,

'We do not know.' And he said to them, 'Neither will I tell you by what authority I am doing these things.'

- The attacks of the chief priests and elders on Jesus were inspired by jealousy and because they felt their own authority was being undermined. In his replies to them Jesus shows his quickness of mind. He always speaks the truth with courage and conviction.
- As we live our Christian lives in an increasingly secular age, we are being asked to witness to the truth that we hold. May we have the confidence to continue doing this in simplicity and sincerity. St Peter tells us we should always have an answer for those who ask us about our faith.

Tuesday 17 December
Matthew 1:1–17
An account of the genealogy of Jesus the Messiah, the son of David, the son of Abraham.

Abraham was the father of Isaac, and Isaac the father of Jacob, and Jacob the father of Judah and his brothers, and Judah the father of Perez and Zerah by Tamar, and Perez the father of Hezron, and Hezron the father of Aram, and Aram the father of Aminadab, and Aminadab the father of Nahshon, and Nahshon the father of Salmon, and Salmon the father of Boaz by Rahab, and Boaz the father of Obed by Ruth, and Obed the father of Jesse, and Jesse the father of King David.

And David was the father of Solomon by the wife of Uriah, and Solomon the father of Rehoboam, and Rehoboam the father of Abijah, and Abijah the father of Asaph, and Asaph the father of Jehoshaphat, and Jehoshaphat the father of Joram, and Joram the father of Uzziah, and Uzziah the father of Jotham, and Jotham the father of Ahaz, and Ahaz the father of Hezekiah, and Hezekiah the father of Manasseh, and Manasseh the father of Amos, and Amos the father of Josiah, and Josiah the father of Jechoniah and his brothers, at the time of the deportation to Babylon.

And after the deportation to Babylon: Jechoniah was the father of Salathiel, and Salathiel the father of Zerubbabel, and Zerubbabel the father of Abiud, and Abiud the father of Eliakim, and Eliakim the father of Azor, and Azor the father of Zadok, and Zadok the father of Achim, and Achim the father of Eliud, and Eliud the father of Eleazar, and Eleazar the father of Matthan, and Matthan the father of Jacob, and Jacob the father of Joseph the husband of Mary, of whom Jesus was born, who is called the Messiah.

So all the generations from Abraham to David are fourteen generations; and from David to the deportation to Babylon, fourteen generations; and from the deportation to Babylon to the Messiah, fourteen generations.

- Matthew, writing for a mainly Jewish audience, gives us this list of the past generations, beginning with Abraham, the father of Israel, to make clear that the coming into the world of Jesus Christ as the Messiah was the fulfilment of a long line of God's prophecies to his people. He introduces this with a reference to Jesus the son of David, because this is the genealogy of Jesus Christ, the royal anointed one.
- We have inherited not only our genes but also our faith from a long line of our ancestors. Do we thank God enough for these people who have passed on so much to us?

Wednesday 18 December
Matthew 1:18–24

Now the birth of Jesus the Messiah took place in this way. When his mother Mary had been engaged to Joseph, but before they lived together, she was found to be with child from the Holy Spirit. Her husband Joseph, being a righteous man and unwilling to expose her to public disgrace, planned to dismiss her quietly. But just when he had resolved to do this, an angel of the Lord appeared to him in a dream and said, 'Joseph, son of David, do not be afraid to take

Mary as your wife, for the child conceived in her is from the Holy Spirit. She will bear a son, and you are to name him Jesus, for he will save his people from their sins.' All this took place to fulfil what had been spoken by the Lord through the prophet:

'Look, the virgin shall conceive and bear a son,
  and they shall name him Emmanuel',

which means, 'God is with us.' When Joseph awoke from sleep, he did as the angel of the Lord commanded him; he took her as his wife.

- This must have been a very difficult time for both Mary and Joseph. It is clear that Joseph puzzled over what he should do and finally resolved on a particular course of action, before the angel intervened. We too are often left by God to puzzle over what we should do in difficult circumstances. Through prayer and careful discernment in the light of the gospels we need to trust that God will show us the way.
- Joseph, like Mary, is specially chosen by God. He is, we read, 'a righteous man', and in his goodness he wants to spare Mary any embarrassment and shame among her neighbours. In his obedience to the message of the angel and in his carrying out of what is being asked of him, he becomes a model for all Christians who seek to do God's will. We ask

for the grace to know and to do God's will and we pray especially for all married couples.

Thursday 19 December
Luke 1:5–25

In the days of King Herod of Judea, there was a priest named Zechariah, who belonged to the priestly order of Abijah. His wife was a descendant of Aaron, and her name was Elizabeth. Both of them were righteous before God, living blamelessly according to all the commandments and regulations of the Lord. But they had no children, because Elizabeth was barren, and both were getting on in years.

Once when he was serving as priest before God and his section was on duty, he was chosen by lot, according to the custom of the priesthood, to enter the sanctuary of the Lord and offer incense. Now at the time of the incense-offering, the whole assembly of the people was praying outside. Then there appeared to him an angel of the Lord, standing at the right side of the altar of incense. When Zechariah saw him, he was terrified; and fear overwhelmed him. But the angel said to him, 'Do not be afraid, Zechariah, for your prayer has been heard. Your wife Elizabeth will bear you a son, and you will name him John. You will have joy and gladness, and many will rejoice at his birth, for he will be great in the sight of the Lord. He must never drink wine or strong drink; even before his birth he will be filled with the Holy Spirit. He will turn many of the people of Israel to the Lord their God. With the spirit and power of Elijah he will go before him, to turn the hearts of parents to their children, and the disobedient to the wisdom of the righteous, to make ready a people prepared for the Lord.' Zechariah said to the angel, 'How will I know that this is so? For I am an old man, and my wife is getting on in years.' The angel replied, 'I am Gabriel. I stand in the presence of God, and I have been sent to speak to you and to bring you this good news. But now, because you did not believe my words, which will be fulfilled in their time, you will become mute, unable to speak, until the day these things occur.'

Meanwhile, the people were waiting for Zechariah, and wondered at his delay in the sanctuary. When he did come out, he could not speak to them, and they realised that he had seen a vision in the sanctuary. He kept motioning to them and remained unable to speak. When his time of service was ended, he went to his home.

After those days his wife Elizabeth conceived, and for five months she remained in seclusion. She said, 'This is what the Lord has done for me when he looked favourably on me and took away the disgrace I have endured among my people.'

- In the story of Zechariah there is a contrast between how Mary believed in the message of the archangel Gabriel and how Zechariah did not. Zechariah is terrified, while Mary is perplexed and ponders the message. Because of his lack of faith he cannot speak about the message. Are there times when our lack of faith keeps us from speaking out the truth when we should and of witnessing to our faith?

Friday 20 December
Luke 1:26–38

In the sixth month the angel Gabriel was sent by God to a town in Galilee called Nazareth, to a virgin engaged to a man whose name was Joseph, of the house of David. The virgin's name was Mary. And he came to her and said, 'Greetings, favoured one! The Lord is with you.' But she was much perplexed by his words and pondered what sort of greeting this might be. The angel said to her, 'Do not be afraid, Mary, for you have found favour with God. And now, you will conceive in your womb and bear a son, and you will name him Jesus. He will be great, and will be called the Son of the Most High, and the Lord God will give to him the throne of his ancestor David. He will reign over the house of Jacob for ever, and of his kingdom there will be no end.' Mary said to the angel, 'How can this be, since I am a virgin?' The angel said to her, 'The Holy Spirit will come upon you, and the power of the Most High will overshadow you; therefore the child to be born will be holy; he will be called Son of God. And now, your relative Elizabeth in her old age has also conceived a son; and this is the sixth month for her who was said to be barren. For nothing will be impossible with God.' Then Mary said, 'Here am I, the servant of the Lord; let it be with me according to your word.' Then the angel departed from her.

- Nothing is impossible with God. Through the power of the Holy Spirit Mary will conceive in her womb a child who will be the Son of God. This mystery is no less awesome than a tiny wafer, through the power of the Holy Spirit, becoming truly the sacred body and blood, soul and divinity of Jesus Christ the Son of God.
- Mary was always a woman of prayer. Her whole life was to be that of the perfect servant of God, living out her 'yes' to God. We too are being asked to interweave our prayer life with how we live our Christian lives so that they become one.

Saturday 21 December
Luke 1:39–45

In those days Mary set out and went with haste to a Judean town in the hill country, where she entered the house of Zechariah and greeted Elizabeth. When Elizabeth heard Mary's greeting, the child leapt in her womb. And Elizabeth was filled with the Holy Spirit and exclaimed with a loud cry, 'Blessed are you among women, and blessed is the fruit of your womb. And why has this happened to me, that the mother of my Lord comes to me? For as soon as I heard the sound of your greeting, the child in my womb leapt for joy. And blessed is she who believed that there would be a fulfilment of what was spoken to her by the Lord.'

- Elizabeth's praise of Mary and her child still find a voice whenever we pray the Hail Mary. There is a great difference between saying prayers and praying prayers. All real prayer is spoken to a person. Whenever we say 'Hail Mary', Mary is immediately attentive to us.
- Enlightened by the Holy Spirit, Elizabeth recognises in Mary the Mother of her God. The Holy Spirit is always active in whatever God wills. It is the same Spirit who has spoken through the prophets. We should often pray to the Holy Spirit for light and guidance in our lives and to serve God in peace and joy.

The Fourth Week of Advent/Christmas

22–28 December 2024

Something to think and pray about each day this week:

Many people find winter difficult; with cold weather and very little sunlight, it can be a tough time. But it is during these weeks that Christians celebrate something amazing: God entering into humanity, putting on skin and living among us as a full human person, in a way that we still find hard to put into words. Jesus was marginalised from the very beginning. Yet he transformed history and continues to transform our lives today.

Into all the harrowing struggles of our world, then and now, God is born. Christ is born again each year in our hearts, if we can make room for him there, and in our world, if we look with awareness in ordinary places. As we light the white candle on the Advent wreath on Christmas morning, let us remember what it represents: the peace, unity and hope for which the world desperately longs.

Tríona Doherty and Jane Mellet,
*The Deep End: A Journey with the
Sunday Gospels in the Year of Mark*

The Presence of God
'Be still, and know that I am God!' Lord, may your spirit guide me to seek your loving presence more and more for it is there I find rest and refreshment from this busy world.

Freedom
By God's grace I was born to live in freedom. Free to enjoy the pleasures he created for me. Dear Lord, grant that I may live as you intended, with complete confidence in your loving care.

Consciousness
How am I today?
Where am I with God? With others?
Do I have something to be grateful for? Then I give thanks.
Is there something I am sorry for? Then I ask forgiveness.

The Word
God speaks to each of us individually. I need to listen, to hear what he is saying to me. Read the text a few times, then listen. (*Please turn to the Scripture on the following pages. Inspiration points are there, should you need them. When you are ready, return here to continue.*)

Conversation
How has God's word moved me? Has it left me cold?
Has it consoled me or moved me to act in a new way?
I imagine Jesus standing or sitting beside me.
I turn and share my feelings with him.

Conclusion
I thank God for these moments we have spent together and for any insights I have been given concerning the text.

Sunday 22 December
Fourth Sunday of Advent
Luke 1:39–45

In those days Mary set out and went with haste to a Judean town in the hill country, where she entered the house of Zechariah and greeted Elizabeth. When Elizabeth heard Mary's greeting, the child leapt in her womb. And Elizabeth was filled with the Holy Spirit and exclaimed with a loud cry, 'Blessed are you among women, and blessed is the fruit of your womb. And why has this happened to me, that the mother of my Lord comes to me? For as soon as I heard the sound of your greeting, the child in my womb leapt for joy. And blessed is she who believed that there would be a fulfilment of what was spoken to her by the Lord.'

- Mary in her kindness hastens to go to her elderly cousin, knowing that she will need help in her pregnancy. Elizabeth recognises the great privilege being given to her. Today we have the privilege of being able to speak to our God and to Mary.
- Elizabeth praises Mary for her great faith in believing the message of the angel. As Jesus grew up in Mary's home from childhood to manhood it must have been extraordinarily difficult for her to realise that this is God. In our prayer let us ponder with Mary over this mystery of our God who

became one of us and who is with us now through his Spirit within us.

Monday 23 December
Luke 1:57–66

Now the time came for Elizabeth to give birth, and she bore a son. Her neighbours and relatives heard that the Lord had shown his great mercy to her, and they rejoiced with her.

On the eighth day they came to circumcise the child, and they were going to name him Zechariah after his father. But his mother said, 'No; he is to be called John.' They said to her, 'None of your relatives has this name.' Then they began motioning to his father to find out what name he wanted to give him. He asked for a writing-tablet and wrote, 'His name is John.' And all of them were amazed. Immediately his mouth was opened and his tongue freed, and he began to speak, praising God. Fear came over all their neighbours, and all these things were talked about throughout the entire hill country of Judea. All who heard them pondered them and said, 'What then will this child become?' For, indeed, the hand of the Lord was with him.

- The name 'John' is of Hebrew origin and means 'God is gracious'. Both Elizabeth and Zechariah recognised that God had indeed been gracious to

them. Our God is continuously gracious to each of us, loving us with an everlasting love.
- In Isaiah we read, 'I have called you by your name, you are mine' (Isaiah 43:1). In the garden of the resurrection, Mary of Magdala recognised Jesus when he called her by her name. Allow him now in your prayer to call you by your name and respond to his immense love for you in whatever way you wish.

Tuesday 24 December
Luke 1:67–69
Then his father Zechariah was filled with the Holy Spirit and spoke this prophecy:
  'Blessed be the Lord God of Israel,
    for he has looked favourably on his people and redeemed them.
  He has raised up a mighty saviour for us
    in the house of his servant David.'
- Zechariah had served his God faithfully in his ministry in the temple. At this initiation rite for his son John, Zechariah's voice is restored to him, and his mind is enlightened by the Holy Spirit. Each of us is also called to a life of fidelity to our God and we have been given the gift of the Holy Spirit

to lead us. How open are we to that same Spirit and do we frequently ask his help in our prayer?

Wednesday 25 December
The Nativity of The Lord
John 1:1–18

In the beginning was the Word, and the Word was with God, and the Word was God. He was in the beginning with God. All things came into being through him, and without him not one thing came into being. What has come into being in him was life, and the life was the light of all people. The light shines in the darkness, and the darkness did not overcome it.

There was a man sent from God, whose name was John. He came as a witness to testify to the light, so that all might believe through him. He himself was not the light, but he came to testify to the light. The true light, which enlightens everyone, was coming into the world.

He was in the world, and the world came into being through him; yet the world did not know him. He came to what was his own, and his own people did not accept him. But to all who received him, who believed in his name, he gave power to become children of God, who were born, not of blood or of the will of the flesh or of the will of man, but of God.

And the Word became flesh and lived among us, and we have seen his glory, the glory as of a father's only son, full of grace and truth. (John testified to him and cried out, 'This was he of whom I said, "He who comes after me ranks ahead of me because he was before me."') From his fullness we have all received, grace upon grace. The law indeed was given through Moses; grace and truth came through Jesus Christ. No one has ever seen God. It is God the only Son, who is close to the Father's heart, who has made him known.

- Today we begin John's Gospel with its Prologue, which used to be read at the end of Mass. Written towards the end of the first century, this gospel is the fruit of much theological reflection. The divinity of Jesus will be emphasised throughout and already we read that all creation comes through Jesus. He is the light come into a darkened world.
- In the Incarnation our God has become one of us and like us in all things but sin. In our prayer now we can relate to him as we would to a really close friend and brother. He loves us and longs for our friendship with him to grow.

Thursday 26 December
St Stephen, Martyr
Matthew 10:17–22

Jesus said to them, 'Beware of them, for they will hand you over to councils and flog you in their synagogues;

and you will be dragged before governors and kings because of me, as a testimony to them and the Gentiles. When they hand you over, do not worry about how you are to speak or what you are to say; for what you are to say will be given to you at that time; for it is not you who speak, but the Spirit of your Father speaking through you. Brother will betray brother to death, and a father his child, and children will rise against parents and have them put to death; and you will be hated by all because of my name. But the one who endures to the end will be saved.'

- Jesus foretells the coming persecutions for his followers but he promises salvation to those who persevere. In one of his letters St Paul tells us that the Lord said to him, 'My grace is sufficient for you.' Lord, you have told us that you will never forsake us or fail us. Help us to have the courage to place our complete trust in you, knowing that your Holy Spirit is within us.

Friday 27 December
St John, Apostle and Evangelist
John 20:2–8

So she ran and went to Simon Peter and the other disciple, the one whom Jesus loved, and said to them, 'They have taken the Lord out of the tomb, and we do not know where they have laid him.' Then Peter and the other disciple set out and went towards the tomb. The two were running together, but the other disciple outran Peter and reached the tomb first. He bent down to look in and saw the linen wrappings lying there, but he did not go in. Then Simon Peter came, following him, and went into the tomb. He saw the linen wrappings lying there, and the cloth that had been on Jesus' head, not lying with the linen wrappings but rolled up in a place by itself. Then the other disciple, who reached the tomb first, also went in, and he saw and believed.

- Jesus gave the first news of his resurrection to the women who had faithfully followed him, even to the foot of the cross. When they go and tell the apostles the news they are not believed. But something of Jesus' own words to them before his death seems to have come back to them and Peter and John run to the tomb to see for themselves.
- It has been said that human beings can take in very little of reality. Are there times when we have wavered in our faith in the love and faithfulness of our God towards us? Our prayer so often can be the prayer of the father whose son the disciples of Jesus were unable to cure: 'Lord, I believe, help Thou my unbelief.'

Saturday 28 December
The Holy Innocents
Matthew 2:13–18

Now after they had left, an angel of the Lord appeared to Joseph in a dream and said, 'Get up, take the child and his mother, and flee to Egypt, and remain there until I tell you; for Herod is about to search for the child, to destroy him.' Then Joseph got up, took the child and his mother by night, and went to Egypt, and remained there until the death of Herod. This was to fulfil what had been spoken by the Lord through the prophet, 'Out of Egypt I have called my son.'

When Herod saw that he had been tricked by the wise men, he was infuriated, and he sent and killed all the children in and around Bethlehem who were two years old or under, according to the time that he had learned from the wise men. Then was fulfilled what had been spoken through the prophet Jeremiah:
'A voice was heard in Ramah,
  wailing and loud lamentation,
Rachel weeping for her children;
  she refused to be consoled, because they are no more.'

- The holy innocents lose their lives because of the hatred of Herod for the child Jesus and so they become martyrs. The long line of martyrs for the sake of Christ continues down to our present day.

- St Joseph, led by the Holy Spirit, protects the child and his mother who have been entrusted to him. We pray to St Joseph, asking him to help us to care for and protect all those for whom we have responsibility.

The First Week of Christmas

29 December 2024–4 January 2025

Something to think and pray about each day this week:

Silvano Fausti SJ wrote a version of the Christmas story that is popular in Italian schools. Caleb was the poorest of the shepherds near Bethlehem that holy night. He had just two sheep. When the angel appeared to the shepherds and told them to go to town to find their Saviour in a manger inside a cave, they quickly gathered up some gifts. Caleb followed them but, being so poor, he had no gift to bring.

When the shepherds reached the cave they proceeded inside, each bearing their gift, kneeling before Jesus. Soon other people arrived, each bringing some gift to honour the sacred child. Caleb remained some way off, too embarrassed to approach the scene empty-handed. Noticing Caleb standing some way off, Mary asked him to come closer, then she placed the baby in his arms, while she arranged the gifts. Caleb's hands were no longer empty. They were, in fact, holding the greatest gift of all.

Gerard Condon, *The Sacred Heart Messenger*,
December 2023

The Presence of God
As I sit here, the beating of my heart,
the ebb and flow of my breathing, the movements of my mind, are all signs of God's ongoing creation of me. I pause for a moment and become aware
of this presence of God within me.

Freedom
Everything has the potential to draw from me a fuller love and life.
Yet my desires are often fixed, caught, on illusions of fulfilment.
I ask that God, through my freedom, may orchestrate my desires in a vibrant loving melody rich in harmony.

Consciousness
I ask, how am I within myself today? Am I particularly tired, stressed, or off-form? If any of these characteristics apply, can I try to let go of the concerns that disturb me?

The Word
I read the word of God slowly, a few times over, and I listen to what God is saying to me. (*Please turn to the Scripture on the following pages. Inspiration points are there, should you need them. When you are ready, return here to continue.*)

Conversation
I begin to talk with Jesus about the Scripture I have just read. What part of it strikes a chord in me? Perhaps the words of a friend or a story I have heard recently will slowly rise to the surface of my consciousness. If so, does the story throw light on what the Scripture passage may be trying to say to me?

Conclusion
Glory be to the Father, and to the Son, and to the Holy Spirit,
As it was in the beginning, is now and ever shall be,
World without end. Amen.

Sunday 29 December
The Holy Family
Luke 2:41–52

Now every year his parents went to Jerusalem for the festival of the Passover. And when he was twelve years old, they went up as usual for the festival. When the festival was ended and they started to return, the boy Jesus stayed behind in Jerusalem, but his parents did not know it. Assuming that he was in the group of travellers, they went a day's journey. Then they started to look for him among their relatives and friends. When they did not find him, they returned to Jerusalem to search for him. After three days they found him in the temple, sitting among the teachers, listening to them and asking them questions. And all who heard him were amazed at his understanding and his answers. When his parents saw him they were astonished; and his mother said to him, 'Child, why have you treated us like this? Look, your father and I have been searching for you in great anxiety.' He said to them, 'Why were you searching for me? Did you not know that I must be in my Father's house?' But they did not understand what he said to them. Then he went down with them and came to Nazareth, and was obedient to them. His mother treasured all these things in her heart.

And Jesus increased in wisdom and in years, and in divine and human favour.

- Jesus mixed so well with relatives and acquaintances that his parents could set out for home trusting he was with their friends. Mary was especially close to Jesus since no man was involved in his conception. So it is like mother, like son. We thank the Father for sending his only Son into our world as a full human being, making it easier for us to relate to him.
- Most of Jesus' life on earth was spent in a small unimportant town doing the very ordinary work of carpentry. We go to God through our humanity. There is a great lesson to be learned here. We can link our own often humdrum lives to his and, like Mary, ponder in prayer the mystery of God with us.

Monday 30 December
Luke 2:36–40

There was also a prophet, Anna the daughter of Phanuel, of the tribe of Asher. She was of a great age, having lived with her husband for seven years after her marriage, then as a widow to the age of eighty-four. She never left the temple but worshipped there with fasting and prayer night and day. At that moment she came, and began to praise God and to speak about the child to all who were looking for the redemption of Jerusalem.

When they had finished everything required by the law of the Lord, they returned to Galilee, to their own town of Nazareth. The child grew and became strong, filled with wisdom; and the favour of God was upon him.

- Anna had lived a very long widowhood and her life was one of fidelity in her worship of God in the temple through prayer and sacrifice. For such a life she is rewarded even on earth by recognising, through the power of the Holy Spirit, the promised Messiah. God will never be outdone in his generosity. May the lives of the saints who have gone before us be an inspiration to us.
- As followers of Jesus Christ may we always strive to put God in the first place in our lives and to give time each day to praying with gratitude and to offering him our sacrifices.

Tuesday 31 December
John 1:1–18

In the beginning was the Word, and the Word was with God, and the Word was God. He was in the beginning with God. All things came into being through him, and without him not one thing came into being. What has come into being in him was life, and the life was the light of all people. The light shines in the darkness, and the darkness did not overcome it.

There was a man sent from God, whose name was John. He came as a witness to testify to the light, so that all might believe through him. He himself was not the light, but he came to testify to the light. The true light, which enlightens everyone, was coming into the world.

He was in the world, and the world came into being through him; yet the world did not know him. He came to what was his own, and his own people did not accept him. But to all who received him, who believed in his name, he gave power to become children of God, who were born, not of blood or of the will of the flesh or of the will of man, but of God.

And the Word became flesh and lived among us, and we have seen his glory, the glory as of a father's only son, full of grace and truth. (John testified to him and cried out, 'This was he of whom I said, "He who comes after me ranks ahead of me because he was before me."') From his fullness we have all received, grace upon grace. The law indeed was given through Moses; grace and truth came through Jesus Christ. No one has ever seen God. It is God the only Son, who is close to the Father's heart, who has made him known.

- Light is a favourite theme in John's Gospel, with emphasis on the enlightenment of our minds that

opens them to the revelation of God. Jesus is the light come into the world to enlighten all who will accept him. He comes to reveal what God his Father is really like. In John 14 we read, 'No one knows the Father except the Son and those to whom the son chooses to reveal him.'
- By reading the gospels frequently we come to know more about the kind of person Jesus is. But it is only through meeting him in heartfelt prayer that we come to know him personally. Lord, may our praying to you each day become a joyful encounter with you.

Wednesday 1 January
Mary, Mother of God
Luke 2:16–21
So they went with haste and found Mary and Joseph, and the child lying in the manger. When they saw this, they made known what had been told them about this child; and all who heard it were amazed at what the shepherds told them. But Mary treasured all these words and pondered them in her heart. The shepherds returned, glorifying and praising God for all they had heard and seen, as it had been told them.

After eight days had passed, it was time to circumcise the child; and he was called Jesus, the name given by the angel before he was conceived in the womb.

- Very few of Mary's words are given in the New Testament. She achieved so much by her silent presence along with her son at many of the key moments in his life, his birth, his first miracle at Cana and his death on the cross. She is for us a model of silent contemplation as she ponders with great faith and devotion the mystery that unfolded before her in the life of her Son.
- The name Jesus is a Greek translation from the commonly used biblical Hebrew Yeshua or Joshua, meaning 'one who saves'. St Peter, speaking to the Jewish authorities after the resurrection, said, 'There is no other name under heaven by which we can be saved.' Let us unite our prayer with the prayer of Jesus to the Father in the Spirit.

Thursday 2 January
John 1:19–28

This is the testimony given by John when the Jews sent priests and Levites from Jerusalem to ask him, 'Who are you?' He confessed and did not deny it, but confessed, 'I am not the Messiah.' And they asked him, 'What then? Are you Elijah?' He said, 'I am not.' 'Are you the prophet?' He answered, 'No.' Then they said to him, 'Who are you? Let us have an answer for those who sent us. What do you say about yourself?' He said,

'I am the voice of one crying out in the wilderness,

"Make straight the way of the Lord",
as the prophet Isaiah said.'

Now they had been sent from the Pharisees. They asked him, 'Why then are you baptising if you are neither the Messiah, nor Elijah, nor the prophet?' John answered them, 'I baptise with water. Among you stands one whom you do not know, the one who is coming after me; I am not worthy to untie the thong of his sandal.' This took place in Bethany across the Jordan where John was baptising.

- John the Baptist always spoke out the truth fearlessly to all who would listen as he called people to repent and turn from sin so that they could be open to the coming of the Messiah. He chastises King Herod for unlawfully marrying his brother's wife and is killed because of this. We are all called to a life of fidelity to the truth.
- John's ministry took place near Bethany, which was a place our Lord later loved to visit as his friends Martha and Mary and their brother Lazarus lived there. Jesus has asked us to make our home in him as he makes his home in us (John 14:23). We pray for the grace to welcome him into our hearts.

Friday 3 January
John 1:29–34
The next day he saw Jesus coming towards him and declared, 'Here is the Lamb of God who takes away

the sin of the world! This is he of whom I said, "After me comes a man who ranks ahead of me because he was before me." I myself did not know him; but I came baptising with water for this reason, that he might be revealed to Israel.' And John testified, 'I saw the Spirit descending from heaven like a dove, and it remained on him. I myself did not know him, but the one who sent me to baptise with water said to me, "He on whom you see the Spirit descend and remain is the one who baptises with the Holy Spirit." And I myself have seen and have testified that this is the Son of God.'

- John the Baptist was someone who was very attuned to the Holy Spirit. He was blessed by God, who had given him his mission, and the Holy Spirit revealed to him in a special way that Jesus was truly the Son of God.
- In John's Gospel (14:21) Jesus has promised that he would reveal himself to us. We pray for the grace to be open to his fulfilment of this promise through our fidelity to daily prayer from the heart.

Saturday 4 January
John 1:35–42

The next day John again was standing with two of his disciples, and as he watched Jesus walk by, he exclaimed, 'Look, here is the Lamb of God!' The two disciples heard him say this, and they followed

Jesus. When Jesus turned and saw them following, he said to them, 'What are you looking for?' They said to him, 'Rabbi' (which translated means Teacher), 'where are you staying?' He said to them, 'Come and see.' They came and saw where he was staying, and they remained with him that day. It was about four o'clock in the afternoon. One of the two who heard John speak and followed him was Andrew, Simon Peter's brother. He first found his brother Simon and said to him, 'We have found the Messiah' (which is translated Anointed). He brought Simon to Jesus, who looked at him and said, 'You are Simon son of John. You are to be called Cephas' (which is translated Peter).

- These two disciples of John had taken to heart his preaching about the One who was to come. Now that he has pointed Jesus out to them they will not miss this chance to meet him. Their response to his invitation to 'Come and see' will change their lives totally. We, too, are invited to 'Come and see.'
- One of the first questions Jesus asks of all his disciples is, 'What are you looking for?' In his *Spiritual Exercises* St Ignatius stresses the importance of the desire for God. 'You will seek Me and you will find Me when you seek Me with all of your heart.'

The Second Week of Christmas

5–11 January 2025

Something to think and pray about each day this week:

The god of Herod in the story of the Magi is tiny, created in Herod's image and likeness. He has made God as tiny as the outreach of his heart.

The God of the Magi was a big god! Big enough to bring the wise men on the long road to Bethlehem. They followed the star of love, goodness, faith, courage, endurance and justice, guided by a star whose light, the light of God, never fails. Their God was big enough to be recognised in a small baby.

The star that guides us is the star of the loves and questions, joys and sorrows of our life's journey. It lives in the hearts of all we meet. Like St Francis of Assisi, we see in a crowd of people not a mob, but the love and image of God multiplied in all. His God was wide, and, like Jesus, his care for God's world went to every person God created, every blade of grass and everything that has life.

Donal Neary SJ, *The Sacred Heart Messenger*,
January 2023

The Presence of God
Dear Jesus, I come to you today longing for your presence. I desire to love you as you love me. May nothing ever separate me from you.

Freedom
Lord, grant me the grace to be free from the excesses of this life. Let me not get caught up with the desire for wealth. Keep my heart and mind free to love and serve you.

Consciousness
Where do I sense hope, encouragement and growth in my life? By looking back over the past few months, I may be able to see which activities and occasions have produced rich fruit. If I do notice such areas, I will determine to give those areas both time and space in the future.

The Word
God speaks to each of us individually. I listen attentively to hear what he is saying to me. Read the text a few times, then listen. (*Please turn to the Scripture on the following pages. Inspiration points are there, should you need them. When you are ready, return here to continue.*)

Conversation
What is stirring in me as I pray? Am I consoled, troubled, left cold? I imagine Jesus standing or sitting at my side, and I share my feelings with him.

Conclusion
Glory be to the Father, and to the Son, and to the Holy Spirit,
As it was in the beginning, is now and ever shall be, World without end. Amen.

Sunday 5 January
Second Sunday of Christmas
(USA The Epiphany of the Lord)
John 1:1–18

In the beginning was the Word, and the Word was with God, and the Word was God. He was in the beginning with God. All things came into being through him, and without him not one thing came into being. What has come into being in him was life, and the life was the light of all people. The light shines in the darkness, and the darkness did not overcome it.

There was a man sent from God, whose name was John. He came as a witness to testify to the light, so that all might believe through him. He himself was not the light, but he came to testify to the light. The true light, which enlightens everyone, was coming into the world.

He was in the world, and the world came into being through him; yet the world did not know him. He came to what was his own, and his own people did not accept him. But to all who received him, who believed in his name, he gave power to become children of God, who were born, not of blood or of the will of the flesh or of the will of man, but of God.

And the Word became flesh and lived among us, and we have seen his glory, the glory as of a father's only son, full of grace and truth. (John testified to him and cried out, 'This was he of whom I said, "He who comes after me ranks ahead of me because he was before me."') From his fullness we have all received, grace upon grace. The law indeed was given through Moses; grace and truth came through Jesus Christ. No one has ever seen God. It is God the only Son, who is close to the Father's heart, who has made him known.

- Because we could not go to God, God came to us and dwelt among us. As Fr Canice Egan SJ put it, 'In the silence of the night Love Itself stole down unseen to embrace the hearts of all.' That the Creator of the universe would deign to take on the nature of his creature and become one of us is so astonishing that we cannot take it in. We ask God to reveal himself to us as he promised he would.

Monday 6 January
The Epiphany of The Lord (Irl)
Matthew 2:1–12

In the time of King Herod, after Jesus was born in Bethlehem of Judea, wise men from the East came to Jerusalem, asking, 'Where is the child who has been born king of the Jews? For we observed his star at its rising, and have come to pay him homage.' When King Herod heard this, he was frightened, and all Jerusalem with him; and calling together all the chief priests and scribes of the people, he inquired of them where the Messiah was to be born. They told him, 'In

Bethlehem of Judea; for so it has been written by the prophet:

"And you, Bethlehem, in the land of Judah,
 are by no means least among the rulers of Judah;
for from you shall come a ruler
 who is to shepherd my people Israel.'"

Then Herod secretly called for the wise men and learned from them the exact time when the star had appeared. Then he sent them to Bethlehem, saying, 'Go and search diligently for the child; and when you have found him, bring me word so that I may also go and pay him homage.' When they had heard the king, they set out; and there, ahead of them, went the star that they had seen at its rising, until it stopped over the place where the child was. When they saw that the star had stopped, they were overwhelmed with joy. On entering the house, they saw the child with Mary his mother; and they knelt down and paid him homage. Then, opening their treasure-chests, they offered him gifts of gold, frankincense, and myrrh. And having been warned in a dream not to return to Herod, they left for their own country by another road.

- The wise men came on a long journey to find the One who was born king of the Jews. Herod urges them to search diligently for him. Where indeed is

God to be found? How earnestly do we seek to find him? The decision to put God and his will in the first place in our life must override all our other decisions, as he can never take second place.
- The wise men were not put off by the humble circumstances in which they found the child-king. It is with the eyes of faith that we must look for God beyond any appearances. 'Lord, I believe, help Thou my unbelief.'

Tuesday 7 January
Matthew 4:12–17.23–25
Now when Jesus heard that John had been arrested, he withdrew to Galilee. He left Nazareth and made his home in Capernaum by the lake, in the territory of Zebulun and Naphtali, so that what had been spoken through the prophet Isaiah might be fulfilled:
'Land of Zebulun, land of Naphtali,
    on the road by the sea, across the Jordan,
    Galilee of the Gentiles [–]
the people who sat in darkness
    have seen a great light,
and for those who sat in the region and shadow
    of death
    light has dawned.'
From that time Jesus began to proclaim, 'Repent, for the kingdom of heaven has come near.'

Jesus went throughout Galilee, teaching in their synagogues and proclaiming the good news of the kingdom and curing every disease and every sickness among the people. So his fame spread throughout all Syria, and they brought to him all the sick, those who were afflicted with various diseases and pains, demoniacs, epileptics, and paralytics, and he cured them. And great crowds followed him from Galilee, the Decapolis, Jerusalem, Judea, and from beyond the Jordan.

- After he had moved from Nazareth to Capernaum, we see Jesus in the full exercise of his public ministry, teaching about the kingdom of God, preaching repentance, and healing all manner of sickness. By reading we come to know about him, but only by meeting him in prayer do we come to know him.
- He is truly the Light come into a world that had such great need of him. As his fame spread throughout Palestine, huge crowds sought him out in their hunger and need. It was said among the people, 'The whole world has gone after him.' We ask for the grace to deepen our desire to know and love him.

Wednesday 8 January
Mark 6:34–44
As he went ashore, he saw a great crowd; and he had compassion for them, because they were like sheep

without a shepherd; and he began to teach them many things. When it grew late, his disciples came to him and said, 'This is a deserted place, and the hour is now very late; send them away so that they may go into the surrounding country and villages and buy something for themselves to eat.' But he answered them, 'You give them something to eat.' They said to him, 'Are we to go and buy two hundred denarii worth of bread, and give it to them to eat?' And he said to them, 'How many loaves have you? Go and see.' When they had found out, they said, 'Five, and two fish.' Then he ordered them to get all the people to sit down in groups on the green grass. So they sat down in groups of hundreds and of fifties. Taking the five loaves and the two fish, he looked up to heaven, and blessed and broke the loaves, and gave them to his disciples to set before the people; and he divided the two fish among them all. And all ate and were filled; and they took up twelve baskets full of broken pieces and of the fish. Those who had eaten the loaves numbered five thousand men.

- Even when it grew late these hungry 'sheep' did not grumble and complain about Jesus preaching to them in this 'deserted place'. They were being fed in their spirits by his words and his message. When the soul is being fed the needs of the body are lessened and we can attend more to the hunger in our souls.

- Our God is a God who provides for all our needs. Let us thank him for everything, but especially for the bread of life that we receive in the Eucharist.

Thursday 9 January
Mark 6:45–52

Immediately he made his disciples get into the boat and go on ahead to the other side, to Bethsaida, while he dismissed the crowd. After saying farewell to them, he went up on the mountain to pray.

When evening came, the boat was out on the lake, and he was alone on the land. When he saw that they were straining at the oars against an adverse wind, he came towards them early in the morning, walking on the lake. He intended to pass them by. But when they saw him walking on the lake, they thought it was a ghost and cried out; for they all saw him and were terrified. But immediately he spoke to them and said, 'Take heart, it is I; do not be afraid.' Then he got into the boat with them and the wind ceased. And they were utterly astounded, for they did not understand about the loaves, but their hearts were hardened.

- It was already late when the crowd were fed and Jesus, worn out by a long day of teaching, felt the need to go and be with his Father in prayer. We know he loved to go aside into a quiet place and, as it were, to recharge his batteries. As Matthew puts

it in his version of this account, 'He went up into the hills by himself to pray.'
- Prayer is always an invitation to sit with the Master and to spend time in his company. Through our imagination we can be with him as he goes to a quiet place to be with his Father. Let us now join this same Jesus who went up into the hills to pray.

Friday 10 January
Luke 4:14–22
Then Jesus, filled with the power of the Spirit, returned to Galilee, and a report about him spread through all the surrounding country. He began to teach in their synagogues and was praised by everyone.

When he came to Nazareth, where he had been brought up, he went to the synagogue on the sabbath day, as was his custom. He stood up to read, and the scroll of the prophet Isaiah was given to him. He unrolled the scroll and found the place where it was written:

'The Spirit of the Lord is upon me,
    because he has anointed me
        to bring good news to the poor.
He has sent me to proclaim release to the captives
    and recovery of sight to the blind,
        to let the oppressed go free,
to proclaim the year of the Lord's favour.'

And he rolled up the scroll, gave it back to the attendant, and sat down. The eyes of all in the synagogue were fixed on him. Then he began to say to them, 'Today this scripture has been fulfilled in your hearing.' All spoke well of him and were amazed at the gracious words that came from his mouth. They said, 'Is not this Joseph's son?'

- It was the custom in Jesus' time for local preachers to be invited to address the people in the synagogue. With great curiosity his former villagers came to listen to him. His gracious words amazed them, but we know from the other versions about this return to Nazareth that jealousy and lack of faith were at work. Do we ever resent the gifts that are given to others, or do we instead give praise and thanks for them?
- As we listen to the words of Jesus in the gospels do we receive them with faith and gratitude? The same Jesus who spoke in that synagogue in Nazareth is with us now in prayer.

Saturday 11 January
Luke 5:12–16

Once, when he was in one of the cities, there was a man covered with leprosy. When he saw Jesus, he bowed with his face to the ground and begged him, 'Lord, if you choose, you can make me clean.' Then Jesus stretched out his hand, touched him, and said,

'I do choose. Be made clean.' Immediately the leprosy left him. And he ordered him to tell no one. 'Go', he said, 'and show yourself to the priest, and, as Moses commanded, make an offering for your cleansing, for a testimony to them.' But now more than ever the word about Jesus spread abroad; many crowds would gather to hear him and to be cured of their diseases. But he would withdraw to deserted places and pray.

- Jesus never refused anyone who came to him with faith asking to be healed. Lepers were not supposed even to approach other people for fear of infecting them. Yet Jesus reaches out and touches and heals the leper. This leper knows he can freely come to Jesus. We know that we too can always come to him to be healed.
- Jesus Christ, yesterday, today, the same for ever, always wants whatever is best for us and gives us healing.

An Advent Retreat

Big words for Advent are to 'stay awake'. We can be awake to the different aspects and mysteries of this time of the year, or sleep through some of them. The point of this season is to be awake to the coming of the Lord, and to notice how we can be reminded of this.

I never liked the 'put Christ back into Christmas', generally delivered in a mournful tone about how we neglect Christ. I prefer – notice Christ in everything of Christmas. Let everything in these weeks remind us of Christ. I have read through some Christmas supplements and not a mention of Christ. But I saw that every picture of a robin, of the snow, of the sleigh and Rudolph can be a reminder of what we are about.

Let everything of these weeks remind us of Christmas: the excitement of the children, the memories of the elderly, the shop visits for gifts, the music on the radio and the last-minute rush. I enjoy the many images of Christmas I see in town. They all remind me of the feast.

Not all our memories are happy – we recall those we miss who have died, particularly in the current year, or other family disappointments. We remember the hardships of the family of Jesus, Mary and Joseph and know their lives and prayer can help us.

An Advent Retreat

There is the strictly religious side. Find time for prayer each day. Look up a website for daily prayer – pray-as-you-go.org, or sacredspace.com. An extra Mass or daily Mass for Advent, a rosary or a decade every day. We find favourite ways of ensuring that the true meaning doesn't pass us by.

We can stay awake, then, to the Lord who comes to us in many ways. In the lifting of the heart about the joy and the meaning of Christmas. In the ways suggested earlier. In all love, and in our care for the needs of the poor. A prayer of 'Come, Lord Jesus' each time we see a crib in town, village and city.

We ask also in the spirit of the loving and giving God – How will my Christmas make another's Christmas a happy one?

Donal Neary SJ

SESSION 1

Invitation to Stillness

As you begin this time of prayer, allow your body to settle into a peaceful and comfortable position. Let your mind settle, putting your preoccupations into God's hands for this time. Notice your breathing, the rhythm of it, and the feel and sound of each breath as you inhale and exhale. With each in-breath, allow yourself to focus on the here and now. With each out-breath let go of any tension or concern you may feel other than being here, still, in this space. John's Gospel tells us that God is with us. God is here now, waiting to fill you with grace and peace.

Reading

Isaiah 25:6–10

On this mountain the LORD of hosts will make for all peoples a feast of rich food, a feast of well-aged wines, of rich food filled with marrow, of well-aged wines strained clear. And he will destroy on this mountain the shroud that is cast over all peoples, the sheet that is spread over all nations; he will swallow up death forever. Then the Lord GOD will wipe away the tears from all faces, and the disgrace of his people he will take away from all the earth, for the LORD has spoken.

It will be said on that day, Lo, this is our God; we have waited for him, so that he might save us. This is the LORD for whom we have waited; let us be glad and rejoice in his salvation. For the hand of the LORD will rest on this mountain. The Moabites shall be trodden down in their place as straw is trodden down in a dung-pit.

Reflect

It's great to celebrate a happy occasion with a good meal. Whether it be a birthday, wedding anniversary, a return from hospital, graduation, new job or retirement, we say things like, 'It's great to be here', or 'It's lovely to have everyone together.' Today's reading from the Book of Isaiah is about a good meal. Unlike some of our meals, everyone – 'all peoples' – is invited. The host is God, and the celebration comes after some bad times. The clue as to the reason for the meal is that 'We rejoice because the Lord has saved us.' Often we are unaware that we need salvation, healing, a lift in life and a love that lasts forever.

Reading

Luke 10:21–24

At that same hour Jesus rejoiced in the Holy Spirit and said, 'I thank you, Father, Lord of heaven and earth, because you have hidden these things from the wise and the intelligent and have revealed them to infants; yes, Father, for such was your gracious will. All things have been handed over to me by my Father; and no one knows who the Son is except the Father, or who the Father is except the Son and anyone to whom the Son chooses to reveal him.'

Then turning to the disciples, Jesus said to them privately, 'Blessed are the eyes that see what you see! For I tell you that many prophets and kings desired to see what you see, but did not see it, and to hear what you hear, but did not hear it.'

Reflect

Many looked forward to the coming of the Messiah, the Christ. He was the hope of the ages to come. But they were dead and gone when he arrived. Jesus praises us that we have seen him. We have seen in him the image of God. As Victor Hugo wrote in *Les Misérables*, if you love, you have seen the face of God. The Jesus we await now is the Jesus we can meet every day – in love, in prayer and in the Eucharist. This is what Pope Francis calls 'social love'. Social love includes our daily relationships, our families and friends, but it also goes beyond them to include a love for the whole world, especially for the poor and those who live in worlds of injustice, war and violence. Our preparation for Christmas puts many challenges to us. The needs of people, both near and far, are great. In Advent we lean into our greatest longings and into the greatest needs of the whole world.

Talk to God

- Lord Jesus, Master of both the light and the darkness, send your Holy Spirit upon our preparations for Christmas. We who have so much to do seek quiet spaces to hear your voice each day; we who are anxious over many things look forward to your coming among us.
- All-powerful God, increase our strength of will for doing good that Christ may find an eager welcome at his coming and call us to his side in the kingdom of heaven, where he lives and reigns with you and the Holy Spirit, one God, for ever and ever. Amen.
- We thank you, Lord, for coming among us, and beginning life as all of us did, in the womb of our mother.

SESSION 2

Invitation to Stillness

As you come into God's presence, know that God is already here, waiting for you. Allow yourself to let go of any tensions you may be carrying in your body, allowing the muscles to relax from your head, neck and face, all down your spine and lower body to your feet. Let your mind settle, putting your preoccupations into God's hands for this time. Listen to the sounds around you, focusing in from those far away to those nearest to you: the sounds within your room, the sound of your own breathing, relaxing as you hear each breath drawn.

Reading

Isaiah 26:1–6

On that day this song will be sung in the land of Judah:

> We have a strong city;
>> he sets up victory
>> like walls and bulwarks.
>
> Open the gates,
>> so that the righteous nation that keeps faith
>> may enter in.
>
> Those of steadfast mind you keep in peace –
>> in peace because they trust in you.
>
> Trust in the LORD for ever,
>> for in the LORD GOD

you have an everlasting rock.
For he has brought low
   the inhabitants of the height;
   the lofty city he lays low.
He lays it low to the ground,
   casts it to the dust.
The foot tramples it,
   the feet of the poor,
   the steps of the needy.

Reflect

We read today about trust. God is 'an everlasting rock'. Rock may seem like an uninviting image of God. Rock can be a stumbling block on a pathway or a beach, or dangerous in the sea. But it is also something of God's creation that lasts. We look at a rock and marvel at how long it has been and will be in place. God is always in place for us; year after year we celebrate that faith in the Advent weeks. We know in bad times we need a rock, and often think of someone as a rock of strength. The rock that is God comes among us, and that's even more surprising.

Reading

Matthew 18:12–14

What do you think? If a shepherd has a hundred sheep, and one of them has gone astray, does he not leave the ninety-nine on the mountains and go in search of the one that went astray? And if he finds it, truly I tell you, he rejoices over it more than over the ninety-nine that never went astray.

Reflect

Jesus would even leave the ninety-nine at risk to find the lost. Not only will he lead the lost one home, but he will carry the lost sheep on his back. This follows another expression of Isaiah, 'he will carry our burdens'. A sheep is heavy and also smelly! The happiness of God is complete when the lost are found. The coming of Jesus is for everyone. The smile of the Bethlehem baby is for the whole world. Maybe Advent can be a time of thinking kindly of everyone and of reconciliation with one another.

Talk to God

- God of power and mercy, open our hearts in welcome. Remove the things that hinder us from receiving Christ with joy so that we may share his wisdom and become one with him when he comes in glory, for he lives and reigns with you and the Holy Spirit, one God, for ever and ever.
- Thank you, Lord, for forgiveness of sin and for healing of the effects of sin. Let your grace strengthen us in living our Christian life.
- Give peace, O Lord, to family, friends and all your people; peace of mind and heart, and peace to the world.

SESSION 3

Invitation to Stillness

As you come into God's presence, know that God is already here, waiting for you. Allow yourself to let go of any tensions you may be carrying in your body, allowing the muscles to relax from your head, neck and face, all down your spine and lower body to your feet. Let the stillness take over and lead you to a space where you can make room for the God of dreams to be with you.

Reading

Isaiah 40:25–31

> To whom then will you compare me,
>   or who is my equal? says the Holy One.
> Lift up your eyes on high and see:
>   Who created these?
> He who brings out their host and numbers them,
>   calling them all by name;
> because he is great in strength,
>   mighty in power,
>   not one is missing.
>
> Why do you say, O Jacob,
>   and speak, O Israel,
> 'My way is hidden from the Lord,
>   and my right is disregarded by my God'?

Have you not known? Have you not heard?
The Lord is the everlasting God,
>   the Creator of the ends of the earth.
He does not faint or grow weary;
>   his understanding is unsearchable.
He gives power to the faint,
>   and strengthens the powerless.
Even youths will faint and be weary,
>   and the young will fall exhausted;
but those who wait for the Lord shall renew
   their strength,
>   they shall mount up with wings like eagles,
they shall run and not be weary,
>   they shall walk and not faint.

Reflect

Here we find God portrayed as the powerful creator – a bit remote. Later in the reading it gets personal. God does not weary in caring for us, giving us strength for the journey. When we allow the mystery of God into our lives, we don't grow weary or tire. This seems very much a big message of Isaiah during these days – if we let God in, then we become strong. Letting God in is allowing the God who comes as a baby into our lives. We can be like Mary – not understanding but pondering the amazement of the Incarnation.

Reading

Matthew 11:28–30

'Come to me, all you that are weary and are carrying heavy burdens, and I will give you rest. Take my yoke upon you, and learn from me; for I am gentle and humble in heart, and you will find rest for your souls. For my yoke is easy, and my burden is light.'

Reflect

We continue receiving the gentle and easy entry of God into the world. Knowing that we need rest and refreshment, God offers that to the soul. Religion sometimes puts heavy burdens on people. True religion begins with the offer from God of unconditional love. The One who loves us with an everlasting love invites us to enjoy the peace and joy of being loved, just like we enjoy the peace and wholeness of being with someone we love.

Talk to God

- Lord God, may we, your people, who look forward to the birthday of Christ experience the joy of salvation and celebrate that feast with love and thanksgiving. We ask this through Christ our Lord.
- Come, Lord Jesus, into this world of yours, which needs your presence and love.
- Give joy and good health, O Lord, to all we meet this day.

SESSION 4

Invitation to Stillness

Come to this time of quiet prayer with a desire to be still and present to God. Perhaps your mind is racing, perhaps this feels like wasted time, when life is so busy. You can offer God the gift of this time and allow the minutes to flow by, without measuring or counting. Breathing in and out, allow yourself to rest in the moment. Can you hear the sounds outside and inside where you are? Perhaps there is a scent from a candle, the freshness of the cool air, or of rain, the feel of warmth against the cold outside. Let your senses draw you into the present moment and the presence of our Creator.

Reading

Zephaniah 3:1–2.9–13

> Ah, soiled, defiled,
> > oppressing city!
> It has listened to no voice;
> > it has accepted no correction.
> It has not trusted in the Lord;
> > it has not drawn near to its God.
>
> At that time I will change the speech of the peoples
> > to a pure speech,
> that all of them may call on the name of the Lord

and serve him with one accord.
From beyond the rivers of Ethiopia
 my suppliants, my scattered ones,
 shall bring my offering.

On that day you shall not be put to shame
 because of all the deeds by which you have
 rebelled against me;
for then I will remove from your midst
 your proudly exultant ones,
and you shall no longer be haughty
 in my holy mountain.
For I will leave in the midst of you
 a people humble and lowly.
They shall seek refuge in the name of the Lord –
 the remnant of Israel;
they shall do no wrong
 and utter no lies,
nor shall a deceitful tongue
 be found in their mouths.
Then they will pasture and lie down,
 and no one shall make them afraid.

Reflect

Prophets often call people back to God or to former promises in life. As the prophet speaks he or she goes back to the promises of God: that in the end God's anger will not last, and God will not desert the people. In our lives we are called to trust in the call of God and the love promised in Baptism; as a community and a society we hear the call to create the new world of justice and peace. When we live in the atmosphere of God, we are at peace and 'can graze and rest'.

Reading

Luke 1:57–66

Now the time came for Elizabeth to give birth, and she bore a son. Her neighbours and relatives heard that the Lord had shown his great mercy to her, and they rejoiced with her.

On the eighth day they came to circumcise the child, and they were going to name him Zechariah after his father. But his mother said, 'No; he is to be called John.' They said to her, 'None of your relatives has this name.' Then they began motioning to his father to find out what name he wanted to give him. He asked for a writing-tablet and wrote, 'His name is John.' And all of them were amazed. Immediately his mouth was opened and his tongue freed, and he began to speak, praising God. Fear came over all their neighbours, and all these things were talked about throughout the entire hill country of Judea. All who heard them pondered them and said, 'What then will this child become?' For, indeed, the hand of the Lord was with him.

Reflect

There was a great sharing of joy when Elizabeth gave birth to John the Baptist. Friends and relations arrived to congratulate her and wonder at the miracle of this birth. One of the marks of love is to be able to share the joys of others. We can think of the joy we all get, even on a bad day, from our children's joy. Christmas joys at best are simple joys: the gift, the touch of love, the thoughtfulness of others, the care for the needy. We take joy especially in the children and have in mind what Elizabeth's visitor believed – that the hand of God is protecting every child and every new life.

Talk to God

- Open our minds to receive the Spirit who prepares us for his coming.
- Open our hearts to welcome the Christ child with love and joy.
- Increase our faith in God among us, Emmanuel. We ask this through Christ our Lord.

Reflection for Advent

Advent is waiting for the birth of Jesus,
but it's a strange waiting:
we are waiting each year for someone we know is here!

We recall in Advent
that the Lord Jesus has come among us, is present all the time
and will come again in glory.

He is the child who is born each year,
for the world always needs its God and Saviour.
He is the child awaited each year,
for our lives are new each year,
and we need him in different ways at different stages of life,
and the world has different needs of God at different times.

We need the child of peace to be born
in our wars and violence,
the child of wisdom in our search for truth and meaning,

the child of gentleness in a world which can be harsh and greedy.